EYE-POPPING
ILLUSIONS
ACTIVITY BOOK

ARCTURUS

ARCTURUS

This edition published in 2015 by Arcturus Publishing Limited
26/27 Bickels Yard, 151–153 Bermondsey Street,
London SE1 3HA

Written by Pat Jacobs
Design and illustration by Dynamo Limited
Edited by Kate Overy, Joe Fullman and Frances Evans
All images supplied by Shutterstock, apart from:
Corbis: p120/Jean Pierre de Mann; p121/ Carlos Barria; p122/ Hendrik
Schmidt; p123/ Nicky Loh, p126 bottom/ Michael Nolan.
iStock: p87/Billyfoto; p76, p77/Silense; p112 top/sdominick; p112
bottom/nicolamargret.

ISBN: 978-1-78212-621-8
CH003798US
Supplier 26, Date 0715, Print Run 4353

Printed in China

CONTENTS

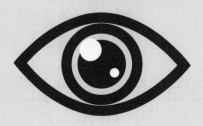

AN INTRODUCTION TO
OPTICAL ILLUSIONS

When we look at things, light passes through the **lens** and enters the eye through the **pupil**. This creates an image on the **retina**, which is like a movie screen at the back of the eye. The retina contains more than 100 million light-sensitive cells called **cone cells** and **rod cells**. Rod cells are good at seeing white light, but can't tell the difference between colors. Recognizing colors is the job of the cones. There are three types—one specializes in seeing red shades, another detects green, and the third is best at seeing blue.

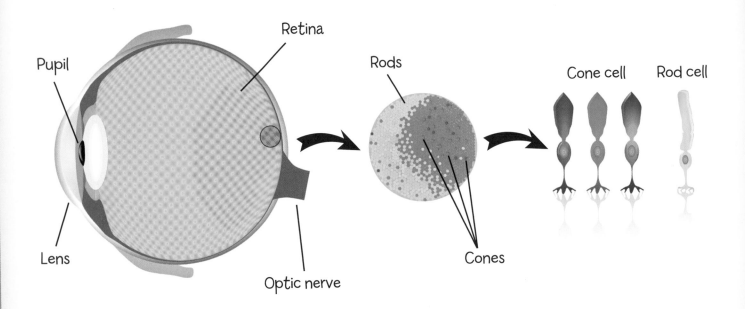

Retina

Pupil

Rods

Cone cell   Rod cell

Lens

Cones

Optic nerve

The optic nerve carries information from the retina to the brain, which makes sense of what the eye is seeing. The images that form on the retina are **two-dimensional**. But because we have two eyes that see things from slightly different angles, the brain can use these two views to work out how far away objects are and produce a **three-dimensional** (3-D) picture.

Our eyes and brain work together so well that we believe what we're seeing is correct, but optical illusions are designed to confuse one or both sides of this perfect partnership. People started to create illusions long before anyone understood how or why they worked. Even today, there are many eye tricks that scientists find difficult to explain.

CHAPTER 1

MOVING IMAGES

Our eyes are always making tiny movements that we are not aware of. The complicated patterns of contrasting colors on the following pages make our eyes move so rapidly that our eyes become overloaded with information. This tricks our brains into seeing movement where there is none.

PULSATING PATTERNS

SEEING IS BELIEVING!

Try staring at the center of these images. They should look as if they are pulsating.

WEIRD!

What happens?

Scientists have come up with theories to explain why our eyes and brain work together to create movement where none exists. It may be that when we stare at something, an **afterimage** remains for a fraction of a second and this overlaps with the picture on the page to produce a rippling effect. Colors that **contrast**, such as black and white, or yellow and blue, make this illusion even more powerful.

It's Bedazzling!

The zigzag images in this pair of glasses appear to be spinning in opposite directions when you glance at them out of the corner of your eye, but they stop as soon as you look directly at them.

WOW!

What happens?

Scientists think that the different levels of brightness in the colors that appear next to one another make us see movement in a stationary image. The colors of the zigzags in these two circles are reversed, which is why they move in opposite directions.

IT'S INCREDIBLE!

The inner and outer circles in this illusion seem to be spinning counterclockwise, while the middle circle spins in a clockwise direction.

I'M A SPIN!

While you read this text, is the pattern below moving? Look closely at the image, and then focus on the page title. When does the pattern move?

Here's another moving illusion. If you look at this page for too long you might start to feel very dizzy.

What happens?

As our eyes try to follow the patterns, they make tiny movements, switching between the lines and colors. This tricks the brain into seeing movement where there isn't any.

ROUND AND ROUND

The spiral pattern on this spinning disk produces an illusion where things seem to be moving away from you.

COOL!

"EYE-POPPING" ACTIVITY!

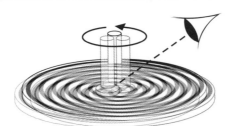

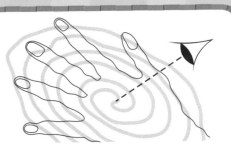

1 Copy the spiral disk onto a piece of cardboard and cut it out. Push a pencil through the center to make a top.

2 Spin the top clockwise. Stare at the center of the spiral for 30 seconds, until you see a "tunnel effect."

3 Quickly look at the back of your hand. The skin will appear to be shrinking inward, away from you.

ROTATING WHEELS

These dancing men look as if they're spinning in different directions. Those in the middle ring are rotating in a clockwise direction and those in the outer and inner circles are going counterclockwise.

The cogs in this brain look as if they're revolving in opposite directions. Perhaps they're trying to puzzle out how this illusion works.

What happens?

If you look closely at the edges of the dancing men and the cogs on the wheels you will see that one side is black and the other is a light color. When the black side is on the left, the image moves in a clockwise direction. When it is on the right, it moves counterclockwise.

FERRIS WHEEL

Complete this picture of a Ferris wheel by drawing in the missing spokes. What happens when you fill in the missing lines?

SCINTILLATING SPIRALS

Does this look like a spiral to you? Try following one of the rings with your finger.

What happens?

The pattern on the **concentric** circles looks like two contrasting cords twisted together, and it was originally called the twisted cord illusion. Combined with the checkered background, this tricks the eye into seeing a phantom spiral.

This illusion also looks like a spiral pattern, but the black bars are actually arranged in concentric circles.

AMAZING!

LOOK INTO MY EYES!

What happens?

This image is a good illustration of the twisted cord effect. It leads the eye from one circle to the next, giving the impression of a spiral pattern. Here, if you follow one of the pointers at the end of the black bars it directs you to the next circle.

Stare into My Eye

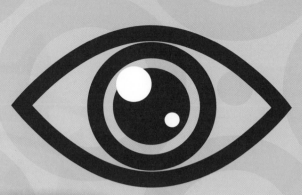

This is a two-in-one illusion. If you look at the center of this image for a while it will appear to move and shimmer. Then follow the ripples just inside the outer edge with your eyes. Can you see them change from a groove to a hump and vice versa?

What happens?

Our eyes are continually making tiny movements that we are not aware of, and this is thought to cause the shimmering effect we see here. We can flip between seeing the ripples around the outside as a groove or a hump in the same way that we can view the book on page 25 as being face up or face down.

UNBELIEVABLE!

Stare at the cross in the center of these circles for ten seconds, then slowly move your head toward and away from the image. The rings should appear to spin in opposite directions.

What happens?

The circles seem to rotate in different directions because the diagonal white bars are each pointing the opposite way.

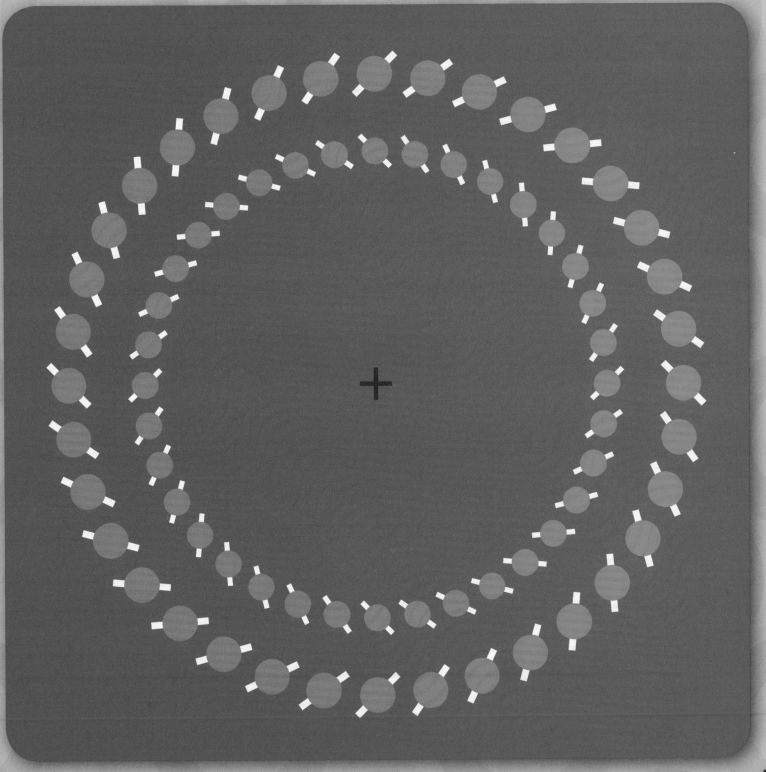

The three illusions on these pages might make you feel a little seasick. Can you see the waves rippling in the image below?

COOL!

HOW DO THEY DO THAT?

The waves in this illusion seem to twist and roll as your eyes pass over the image.

AMAZING!

As you look at this image, the whole design appears to ripple. It is called the floating rice illusion and was created by Akiyoshi Kitaoka, a Japanese master of visual art.

MESMERIZING MOTION

These two pictures show how illusions can be used creatively as part of a scene. The leaves on this tree look as if they are moving if you glance at them out of the corner of your eye.

SOMETHING FISHY!

In this aquatic scene something fishy is going on. The ocean is alive with swimming fish! Can you see them moving?

SEEING IS BELIEVING

MOVIE TIME

Animation creates moving images by displaying a series of images so quickly that the brain blends them together to give the illusion of continuous motion. A flip book is a very simple form of animation. Here's how to make your own. You will need a booklet of sticky notes or a small notepad.

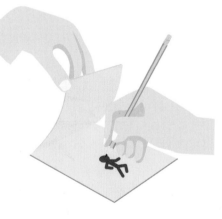

1 Copy the first running figure shown above onto page one of the pad.

2 On page two, in the same position on the page, draw the second running figure and so on until you have copied all the figures.

3 Repeat the figures until all the pages of your pad are filled. Then quickly flick through them to see your figure running.

CHAPTER 2

MIND CONTROL

The illusions in this part of the book show how the eyes and brain can be confused and make us see things that are not really there.

ALL CHANGE

Some optical illusions can make images change before your very eyes. Hold this book horizontally at eye level and look at the two fishing rods, following the direction of the arrow at the bottom of the page. You should see a third rod rising up out of the page.

COOL!

What happens?

When you look at the rods from this viewpoint, the images from each eye join together and create a third image between the two.

24

Is this book face up or face down? This is an example of an image that can be seen by the brain in two different ways.

Hold this page at arm's length and slowly move the book toward your face. What happens to the birds?

What happens?

When you move the page closer to your face, the images of the birds and the cage overlap so the birds appear to be inside the cage.

SHAPE SPINNER

"EYE-POPPING"

1 Draw a circle on a piece of cardboard. Copy the design shown here onto the cardboard and cut it out.

2 Push a pencil through the center to make a toy top. Spin the spinner and see what happens. The small circles should turn into large concentric circles.

MISSING PIECE?

Someone has taken a slice from this cake. To find the missing piece, turn the book upside down.

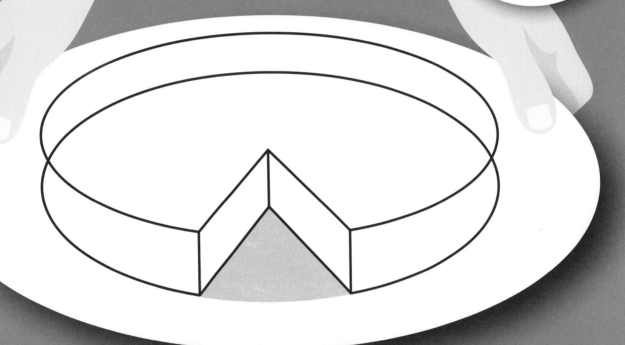

What happens?

Although the picture is exactly the same, the cake is now upside down on the plate. Our brains are not used to seeing a cake from this angle, so we make sense of the image by assuming that it shows a single slice in a cake tin.

AMAZING!

NOW YOU SEE IT...

Do you see a pattern of stars or stacks of cubes when you look at this page? The longer you look at it, the more you will change your mind.

What do you see when you look at this image? Is it a pattern of concentric circles, **tesselated** triangles, or six-point, curve-sided stars?

What happens?

These illusions show how flexible our brains can be. We can see these images in several different ways and flip between them, even though the picture does not change.

Twisted CIRCLES

These may not look like circles, but they are actually perfectly round. Try putting a piece of tracing paper over the image and drawing around the circles using a compass if you don't believe it.

What happens?

The pattern on the circles confuses the eye in the same way as the twisted cord illusion on page 14. At the same time, the radiating background distorts our view of the circles even more.

Hole in Hand

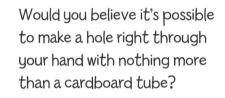

Would you believe it's possible to make a hole right through your hand with nothing more than a cardboard tube?

You'll need a cardboard tube (from a roll of paper towels, for example) or a piece of paper rolled into a tube.

Hold the tube in front of one eye and look at something in the distance. Cover your other eye with the palm of your free hand. Slowly slide this hand away from you, along the side of the tube, keeping your palm flat. You should be able to see through what appears to be a large hole in your hand.

"EYE-POPPING" ACTIVITY!

AWESOME!

What happens?

This illusion plays tricks with your **binocular vision**. One eye registers the hole in the tube on the same part of the retina as the other eye registers the hand. Your brain thinks that the two images are coming from the same place, so you see the tube running through your hand.

KEEP ON STARING...

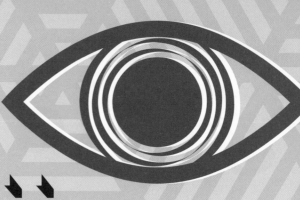

Stare at this design for a while under a bright light. What do you see?

What happens?

You should see flashing white stars bouncing among the black stars.

triangle TROUBLE

Use a pencil and ruler to draw over the dotted lines. Can you see an upside-down white triangle in the center of the image? This illusion is known as Kanizsa's triangle.

What happens?

Although only the corners of the ghostly triangle exist, our brains automatically fill in the sides to complete the image and trick us into seeing something that isn't really there.

HOW DO THEY DO THAT?

GHOSTLY VISAGE...

Stare at this lady's nose for 30 seconds. Now close your eyes and tilt your head back. After a few seconds, a ghostly face should appear before you.

UNBELIEVABLE!

What happens?

This is called an **afterimage**. As you stare at the picture, the parts of your eye that respond to light become tired. Those that react to the brightest light get tired more quickly, so when you close your eyes, you see a **negative** afterimage in which the brightest parts appear dark and the dark parts look white.

WACKY!

TWO IN ONE

The thaumatrope was a popular toy at the end of the 19th century. It consists of some cardboard with a picture on each side attached to two pieces of string. When the strings are twirled, the two images combine to make a single picture. Here's how to make your own.

1 *Cut out a square of cardboard and punch a hole on the left and right sides. Thread string through each hole and tie the ends of each one so you have two loops. Draw a fish bowl on one side and a small fish in the center of the other.*

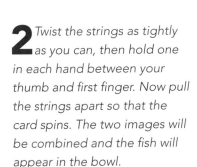

2 *Twist the strings as tightly as you can, then hold one in each hand between your thumb and first finger. Now pull the strings apart so that the card spins. The two images will be combined and the fish will appear in the bowl.*

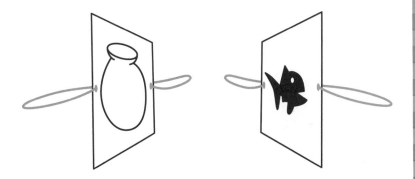

Did you know?
The word thaumatrope comes from Greek words meaning "wonder turner."

FLOATING SAUSAGE

WACKY!

Place the tips of your index fingers together and hold them about 6 inches in front of your face at eye level. Look past your fingers at something 5 or 6 feet away. Pull your fingers about half an inch apart and a floating sausage shape with a nail at each end will appear. By moving your fingers closer together or farther apart you can change the size of the sausage.

"EYE-POPPING" ACTIVITY!

What happens?

When you focus on something in the distance, your brain overlaps the images in the foreground, creating the floating finger sausage. If you look directly at your fingers, the sausage disappears.

CHAPTER 3

CRYPTIC COLOR

The next puzzles are based on the way the cone cells in our eyes recognize color. This changes according to the background, so two identical colors can look completely different depending on the colors surrounding them.

COLOR CONTRAST

What happens?

This illusion is interesting because it doesn't follow the normal rules. Colors seen on a lighter background usually look darker than those on a darker background. Therefore we would expect the gray bands sandwiched between the white bars to look darker than those sandwiched between the black bars. Experts cannot agree why the opposite happens with this image.

Look carefully at this image, called White's illusion. Is the **vertical** gray band on the left of this picture lighter than the band on the right? In fact, they are exactly the same shade.

DIFFERENT SHADES

AMAZING!

Look at the rows of diamonds that make up this pyramid. Does each row look darker than the row above it? Actually, all the diamonds are identical—although it may be hard to believe!

What happens?

Each diamond is darker at the top than at the bottom. This color contrast tricks the brain into believing that the diamonds are different shades.

SEEING IS BELIEVING

39

COLOR CONUNDRUM

How many different shades do you see in this image? Most people see two shades of pink and two shades of green, but take a closer look—there is just one shade of pink and one of green.

What happens?

Our brains see colors differently according to the colors alongside them. When the pink and green squares are surrounded by white squares, they appear to be lighter.

How many shades of green are there in this image? Believe it or not, there's just one.

WEIRD!

TRUE BLUE?

It's clear that the blue squares in these two grids are exactly the same color, but you can create your own illusion by making the right-hand grid look darker.

1 Using a ruler and a black felt-tip pen, draw a black frame around the grid on the right and fill in all the white lines with black, so each square has a black border.

2 Now compare the two grids. Do the blue squares in the right-hand grid still look the same shade as those on the left?

COLOR CONFUSION!

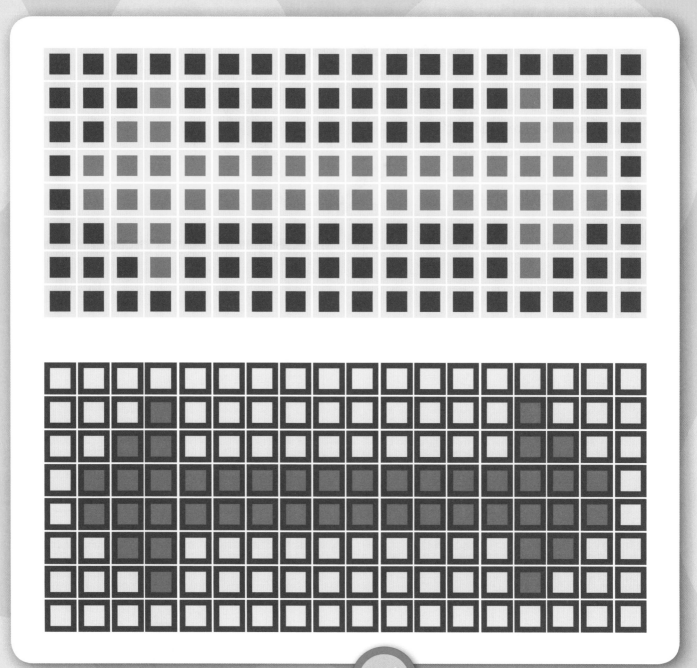

These arrows appear to be different colors, but the only difference between them is the color of the borders surrounding the red squares.

What happens?

This is an example of **color assimilation**. The red squares that are surrounded by yellow frames have becomed tinged with yellow, making them look orange. The red squares that are surrounded by blue have taken on a bluish tinge, so they appear to be a deeper shade of red.

can you spot it?

Move your eyes around this picture. Can you see red dots appear and disappear where the corners of the squares meet (the intersections)? If you stare directly at an intersection the red dot does not appear!

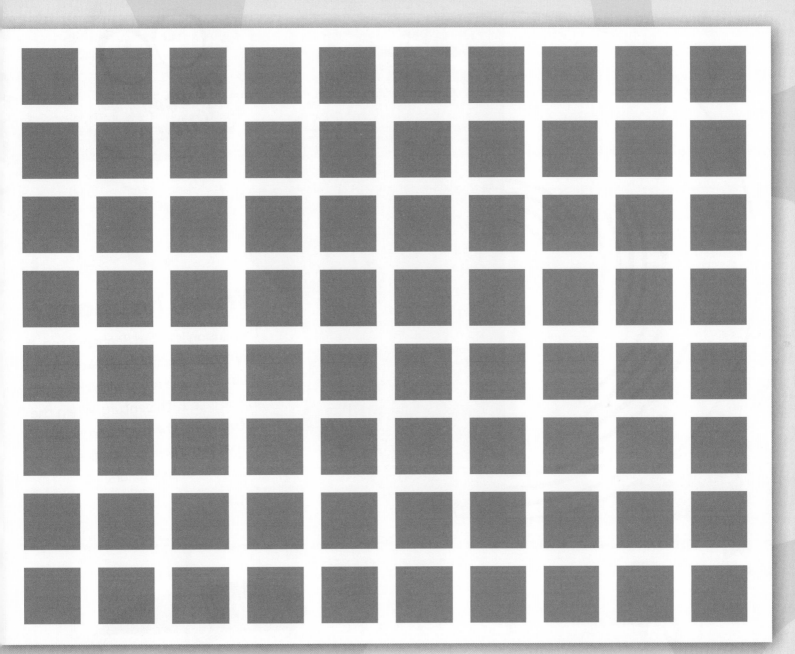

What happens?

When you move your eyes over the image, the way your eyes respond to the different amounts of light coming from the red squares and white lines means that you perceive the "ghost" of a red dot at the intersections.

SPOOKY!

CREATING COLOR

You can turn black and white into color with this spinner.

"EYE-POPPING" ACTIVITY!

What happens?

This illusion is called Benham's top. It is named for English toymaker Charles Benham, who sold a top with this pattern in the late 19th century. When the top spins, the black and white patterns produce an illusion of pale colors.

1 Copy the disk design shown above onto some cardboard and carefully cut it out.

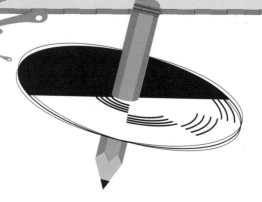

2 Push a pencil through the center to make a spinner. As the disk spins you will see concentric rings tinged with colors.

CHAPTER 4

PECULIAR PICTURES

Our brains usually decide what we're looking at within a split second, but the illusions in this part of the book can be seen in two different ways. We can flip between the two alternative images, but we cannot see both at the same time.

IS IT OR ISN'T IT?

Do you see an old woman or a young girl when you look at this picture? It all depends whether you see an eye or an ear in front of her hair.

WEIRD!

What happens?

This type of illusion proves that we see with our brains as well as with our eyes. Although the picture remains the same, our brains flip between seeing one image and then the other.

SEEING IS BELIEVING

Is this a rabbit looking to the right or a duck facing left?

Something about this elephant isn't quite right. Can you count how many legs it has? Some say four, others say six, or perhaps it's eight.

SPOOKY!

What happens?

Although we know that elephants have four legs, here the tops of the legs are not all connected to the feet. Our brains are confused because we recognize objects by their outer edges. We automatically try to build a 3-D picture of an elephant in our minds, but it is impossible.

I CAN SEE THE BEGINNING...

How many cats can you see here? It depends whether you are counting the heads and front legs of the purple cats or the tails and back legs of the pink cats—or both.

HOW DO THEY DO THAT?

AWESOME!

WHERE WILL IT END?

WACKY!

Which hind legs and tails belong to which dogs in this canine line up? If you follow the lines you will see that the answer is none.

SEEING IS BELIEVING

WHICH WAY UP?

LOOK INTO
MY EYES!

The grumpy old lady on the left can be transformed into a smiling princess just by turning the image upside down. These topsy-turvy images became very popular in the late 19th century, when they often appeared on postcards.

AMAZING!

BACK TO FRONT?

This strange picture shows two people facing in opposite directions. The young woman is looking to the left and the man with the mustache is looking right. Try creating some topsy-turvy or double-faced characters of your own.

SPOOKY!

FANTASTIC FACES

Take a look at this picture below. Is this an image of a golden chalice or the silhouettes of two heads face to face? It's up to you to decide...

FRUIT FACE

Can you see two faces in this apple core?

What happens?

These two illusions are examples of the brain's ability to flip from one view of an image to another, even though the picture itself does not change.

WACKY!

FACE TO FACE

Create your own illusion by drawing a mirror image of the silhouette shown here. What do you think you will create? A vase? A candlestick? Get drawing to find out.

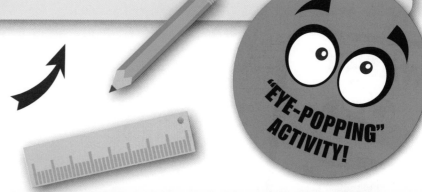

"EYE-POPPING" ACTIVITY!

CHAPTER 5

SHAPES, SIZES, AND ANGLES

We're usually very good at judging distances, sizes, and shapes because our brains are trained to work out how things relate to one another. These illusions use clever tricks to fool the brain, so not everything you see here is as it appears.

HOW BIG?

Which of these two yellow circles is bigger? Measure them both with a ruler to see if you are right.

AMAZING!

What happens?

Our brains automatically compare the size of the yellow circles to the size of the gray circles surrounding them and assume that the one on the left is smaller and the one on the right is larger.

Which of the three men in the picture above is the tallest? The answer is that all three are exactly the same size. If you don't believe it, try measuring them with a ruler.

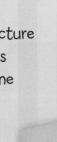

WEIRD!

UNBELIEVABLE!

What happens?

This illusion makes use of perspective lines to suggest distance. Our brains know that objects in the distance look smaller. Therefore we automatically assume that the figure farthest away is much larger. This is a variation of the Ponzo illusion on page 71.

TABLE TRICK

Do these tables appear to be different sizes? It's hard to believe, but the width of the tabletop on the left is the same as the length of the tabletop on the right. And the length of the tabletop on the left is the same as the width of the tabletop on the right. Measure the yellow and blue lines on the tables below to check it out for yourself.

IT'S INCREDIBLE!

What happens?

Because of the way the legs and sides of the tables have been drawn, our brains judge that the table on the left is longer and the one on the right is wider based on our past experiences of angles and perspective.

FOOLING THE EYE ?

Which of these lines is longer: A to B or B to C? Measure them to check your answer.

AMAZING!

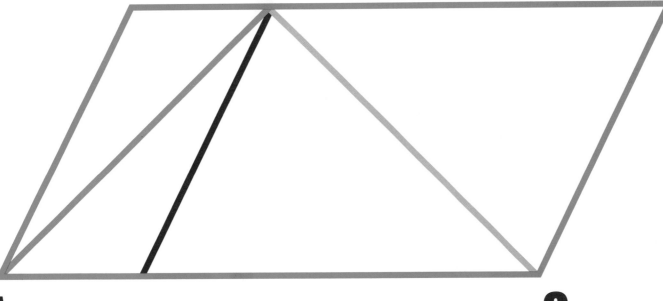

B.

A.

C.

SEEING IS BELIEVING

What happens?

If you trace the triangle made up by the lines AB, BC and AC, it is obvious that the two lines are the same length. It is the angle of the other lines that confuses the eye.

A QUESTION OF SIZE

Are these two curved segments different sizes? Trace one and compare them.

What happens?

The segments are identical, but our brains compare the shorter arc at the bottom of the top segment to the longer arc at the top of the segment below. This illusion was first discovered by German psychologist Wilhelm Wundt in the 19th century.

Are these white bars the same size? Measure them to find out.

What happens?

This illusion shows how easily the brain can be fooled. The bar on the right looks larger simply because the purple frame surrounding it is shorter.

Which of these two vertical lines is longer? Surprisingly, they are both the same length.

SPOOKY!

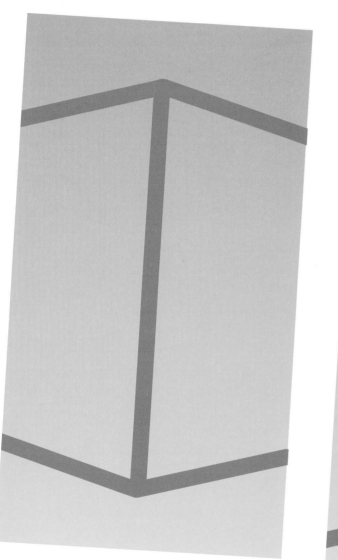

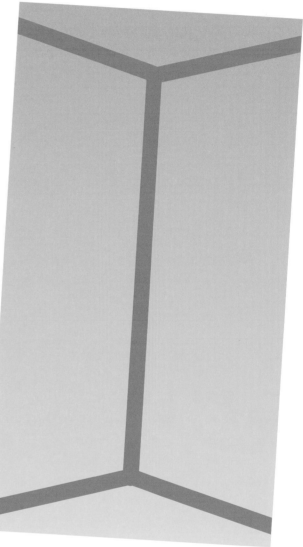

HOW DO THEY DO THAT?

What happens?

Because the overall length of the image on the right is longer than the one on the left, the brain is fooled into thinking that the vertical line is longer on that side.

POINT OF VIEW

Complete this illusion by drawing two vertical lines over the dotted guides. Now, without using a straight edge, guess which line is a continuation of line C? Is it A or B?
If you guessed A, you are incorrect. Scientists are still not really sure why this old illusion works. It could be because the two vertical lines confuse our rough calculation of the angle of line C.

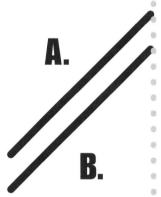

C.

A.

B.

Are the long lines here **parallel** to one another? Trace over them using a ruler to find out.

What happens?

The different angles of the shorter lines cause a tilting effect, which confuses us into thinking that the lines are not parallel.

STRAIGHT OR BENT?

Do you think the two purple lines are straight or do they bulge in the middle? Use a straight edge to check for yourself.

WEIRD!

What happens?

The lines radiating out from the center confuse the brain into thinking that the two vertical lines are curving outward.

LYING LINES

Are the vertical and **horizontal** yellow and black lines straight or wobbly? Surprisingly, they are all straight.

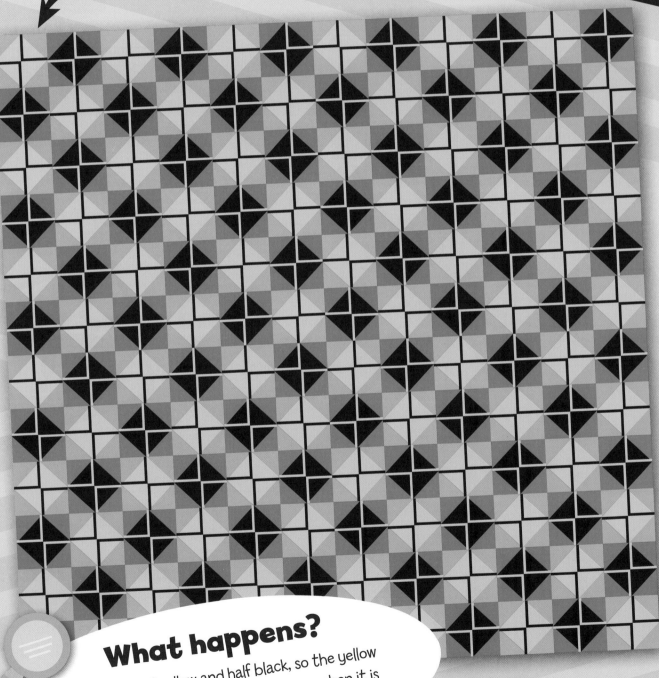

What happens?

Each line is half yellow and half black, so the yellow or black part of the line cannot be seen when it is printed on the matching color square.

WIBBLY-WOBBLY WALLS

Draw in the horizontal lines on this wall by joining the dots with a pen and a ruler. Now look closely at the wall. Are the lines at an angle to each other or are they parallel?

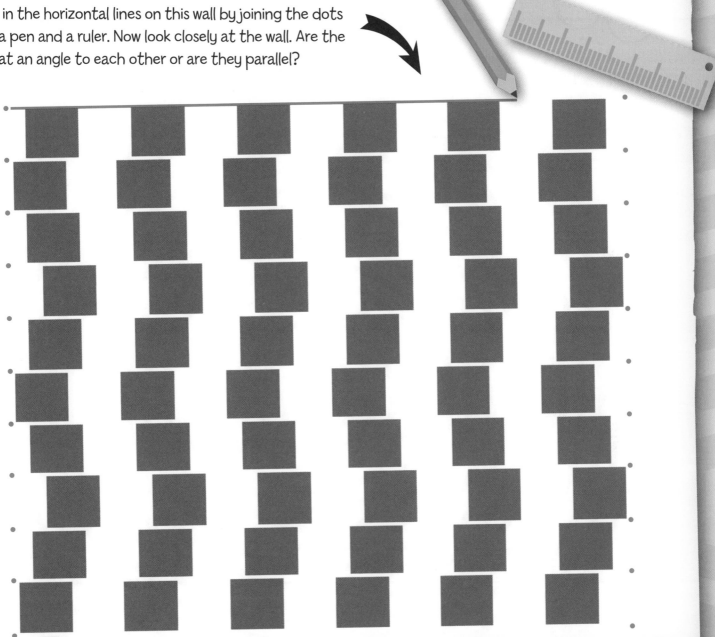

What happens?

When alternating bricks of dark and light colors are stacked in an unaligned pattern, the lines between them seem to tilt toward each other.

"EYE-POPPING" ACTIVITY!

Bending
THE TRUTH

Are the sides of this square straight or curved?

What happens?

The sides of the square are perfectly straight, but the circles in the background make the lines look curved.

Are the lines in this checkerboard pattern all straight and parallel? Check them out using a straight edge.

What happens?

You see the lines as wavy because of the positioning of the little blue and white squares within the larger squares. These mislead the parts of the brain that use the edges of an object to decide what it is. Note how some of the small squares are positioned differently to give the impression that the checkerboard is bulging outward in the center.

Seeing Isn't Always Believing

In these two pictures of the Leaning Tower of Pisa, the tower on the right seems to be leaning more than the tower on the left, even though the images are identical.

What happens?

Our brains treat these two pictures as if they were a single image. According to the normal rules of perspective, the towers would appear to lean toward each other when viewed from below and our brains would correct this so we would see them as parallel towers. As these two are both leaning in the same direction, our brains assume that they are not parallel to each other.

Which fish is the bigger of the two? In fact, they are both the same size.

What happens?

The bottom fish looks larger because it fills the space between the two lines. As the lines stretch further apart, the fish above appears to be smaller because there is more space on either side of it.

UNBELIEVABLE!

OUT OF PERSPECT1VE

The circle at the center of the triangle and the circle below it are identical, so why do they look different?

What happens?

This is another example of an illusion where the background pattern distorts our view of the object in the foreground.

SPOOKY!

Does this look like a perfect square or does it seem to be distorted?

What happens?

The angled lines in the background give an illusion of perspective. This makes us see the square as distorted.

Which of these two yellow lines is longer? Check them with a ruler to make sure.

HOW DO THEY DO THAT?

What happens?

Although the two yellow lines are the same size, our brains assume that the top line is farther away because of the black lines, which look like a railroad track extending into the distance. Therefore we think that the top line must be larger than the bottom line. This is called the Ponzo illusion.

ON BALANCE...

Complete the pattern of diagonal lines on the top beam. Do the beams look parallel to you, or is one end weighed down by the blue triangle?

What happens?

The two beams are parallel to one another but one looks tilted because the diagonal lines running in opposite directions trick the eye.

CHAPTER 6

IMPOSSIBLE OBJECTS

By playing with the normal perspective, shapes, and arrangements of objects, artists create pictures of things that could never exist in the real world. English artist William Hogarth was one of the first to create an impossible landscape in 1754 with his engraving called "Satire on False Perspective."

WHICH WAY AROUND?

Do you think you would be able to make this triangle from building blocks?

COOL!

What happens?

This illusion, sometimes called the Penrose triangle, could not exist as a 3-D object because it is shown from several angles at the same time.

CUBE
CONUNDRUM

AWESOME!

Is this object a flat hexagon or an impossible cube?

Intriguing SHAPES

Here is another shape that can exist only on paper. Follow the shape with your finger to check that it is impossible.

Tell me more

Swedish artist Oscar Reutersvärd is known as "the father of the impossible figure." He created the Penrose triangle on page 76 and many other impossible objects.

IT'S IMPOSSIBLE...

Join the dots to finish this impossible object, then color the area inside the dotted line red to complete it .

COOL!

SHIFTING SHAPES

This wooden object would challenge even the most skillful carpenter.

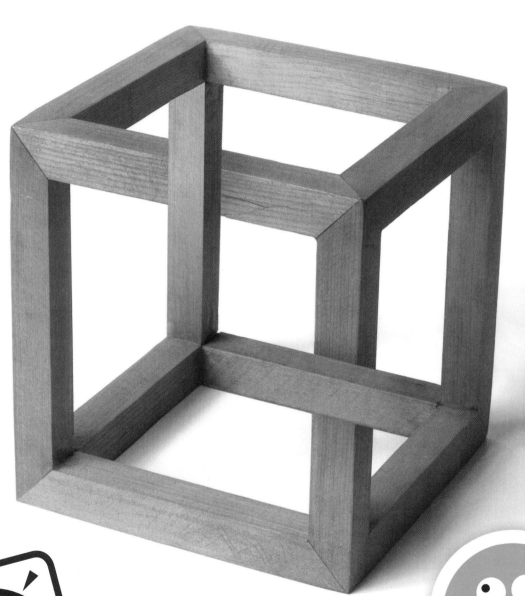

SPOOKY!

It's impossible to tell which way this strange wooden object is facing.

WACKY!

HOW DO THEY DO THAT?

HOW DO THEY DO THAT?

"EYE-POPPING" ACTIVITY!

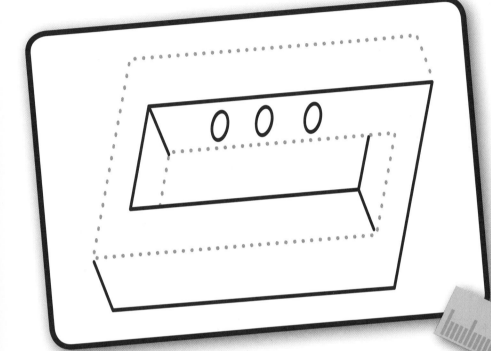

Trace over the dotted lines to complete these impossible objects. Are the circles on the inside or outside of this figure?

This impossible fork is known as the devil's pitchfork, or a poiuyt. This last name was invented by 'Mad' Magazine and is made up of the letters of the third row of the keyboard typed from right to left.

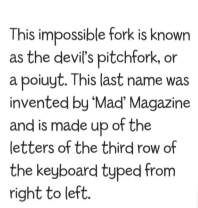

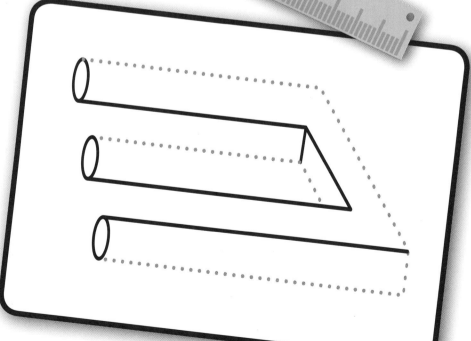

Now try to color it in. What happens?

BUILD THE IMPOSSIBLE?

COOL!

SEEING IS BELIEVING

Could you construct this confusing structure from building blocks? You won't be able to, of course, because it's impossible. The trick is that the long beam across the top is not actually attached to the back column. If you position the blocks carefully, then close one eye and squint at it from a particular angle, it will look very convincing.

Dimension

Here is another intriguing object that could not exist in real life. The longer you look at it, the more confusing it becomes.

AMAZING!

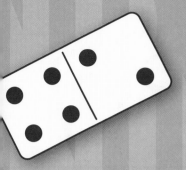

DOMINO DOUBT!

These dominoes seem to be lying on a flat table, so how can they appear to step up and down?

WEIRD!

STAIR CRAZY

COOL!

Try following these strange staircases with your finger. Would you be moving upward each time you took a step?

Tell me more

The picture above is by Dutch artist M. C. Escher, who is famous for his drawings of impossible constructions. It features a world where the normal rules of gravity do not apply. The more you look at it, the more you realize how "impossible" it is.

IT'S INCREDIBLE!

Daft
DESIGNS

Would you want to put an expensive vase on this impossible shelf? Is the cup hanging from a hook on the inside or the underside of the shelf?

WEIRD!

This 3-D illustration shows an impossible arrangement of linked cogwheels.

HOW DO THEY DO THAT?

There is something strange about the perspective of this engine and boiler.

WOW!

STRANGE SCIENCE

This picture of a chemistry experiment looks quite normal at first glance, but a closer look reveals that the arrangement of the equipment is impossible.

Weird WORLD

Can you see a face hidden in this coastal scene? Here's a tip - try turning the book sideways.

SPOOKY!

NEVER ENDING PATH...

This may look like yet another impossible object, but it is one that you can recreate. The Möbius strip, also called a magic circle, is a loop with just one surface and one edge. It sounds impossible, but here's how to make one.

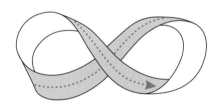

"EYE-POPPING" ACTIVITY!

The Möbius strip is named for the German mathematician who discovered it in 1858.

1 Cut a long strip of paper, keeping the width even.

2 Holding one end in each hand, give the strip a half twist and tape the two short ends together.

3 You now have a Möbius strip. To prove that your loop has just one surface, take a pen and draw a line along the center of the strip.

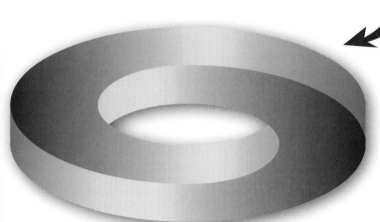

What happens if you cut the strip in half lengthwise, along the dotted line? Do you end up with two separate loops as you might expect?

CHAPTER 7

3-D ILLUSIONS

Because we live in a 3-D world, our brains are used to changing the two-dimensional images that form in our eyes into 3-D objects. Although the following pictures are completely flat, our brains still convert them into 3-D, so they appear to be popping out of the page.

LEAPING OUT

This powerful illusion is so effective that the cube appears to be floating above the checkered background.

What happens?

The change in the size and angle of the white shapes in this illusion make it look as if the center of the image is bulging out from the page.

UNBELIEVABLE!

COOL!

TO AND FRO

Are you looking at these cubes from above or below? How quickly can your brain switch between seeing them from one angle, then from the other?

HOW DO THEY DO THAT?

Puzzling PATTERNS

Are these flat patterns or 3-D images?
The shading would lead you to think that
they are 3-D, but how do they fit together?

WEIRD!

FLIP-FLOPPING

Some 3-D images can be seen in two ways. Are these two illusions cones coming toward you or tunnels going away from you?

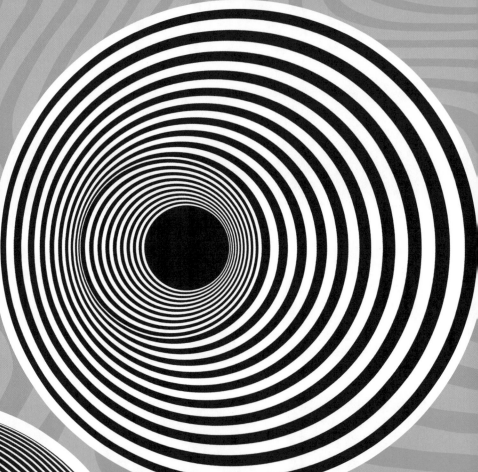

LOOK INTO MY EYES!

Is the center of this pattern the top of a pyramid or the end of a long corridor?

Are you looking at this cylinder from the left or from the right?

The Necker CUBE

SPOOKY!

Look carefully. Is the red dot on the corner of the cube that is nearest to you or on the one that is farthest away?

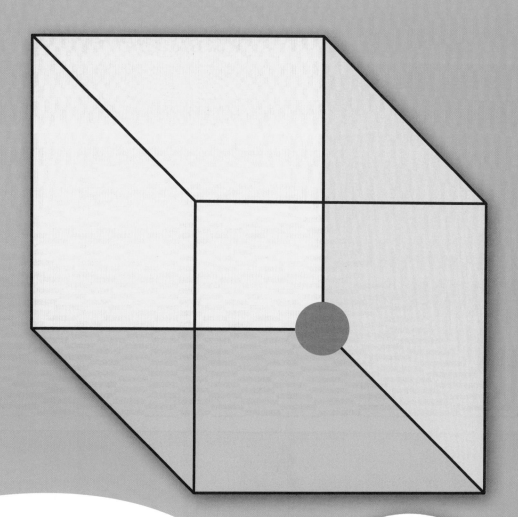

What happens?

Your brain recognizes this two-dimensional drawing as a cube, but there is not enough information for it to work out which surface is at the front. Therefore it flips between seeing it one way and then the other.

BUILDING BLOCKS

Complete this illusion by drawing over the dotted lines. Is this structure coming out of the page toward you or tilting backward?

COOL!

HIDDEN PICTURES!

SPOOKY!

Take a look at these three images. What can you see? Nothing other than a colored pattern? Then look again. There is a three-dimensional picture hidden in each one. A 3-D picture hidden within another image like this is called a **stereogram**.

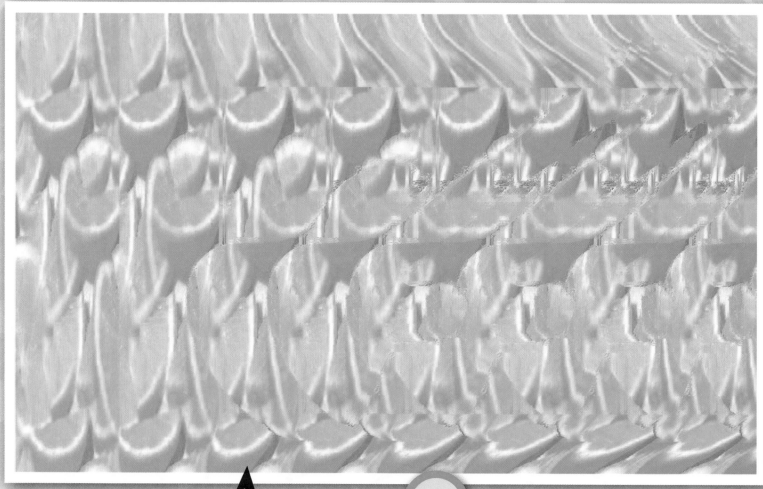

Can you see a guitar?

To see the 3-D pictures you need to relax your eyes and try to look through the page, as if you were staring at something in the distance. At first, it may take some time for your brain to adjust. But after a while you should be able to see an image emerge.

What happens?

Because our eyes are spaced apart, we see the world from two slightly different angles. A stereogram mimics this effect by incorporating two images taken from different angles. Our brains then combine the two pictures to create a 3-D image.

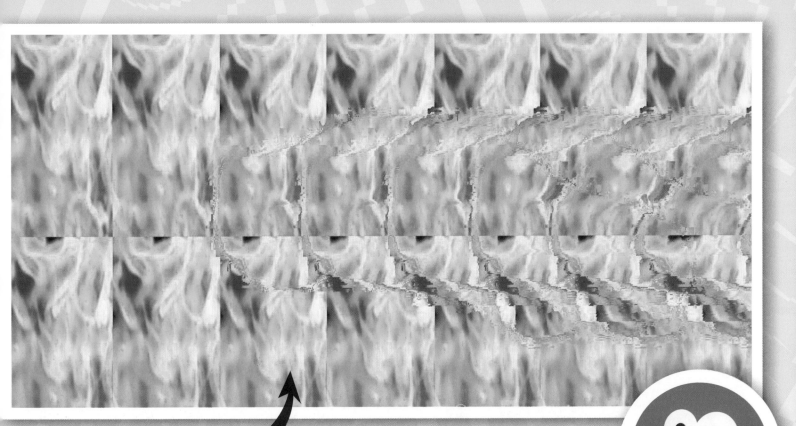

Can you see a car?

Can you see a cube ?

HIDDEN PICTURES!

Tell me more

Most people have to train their eyes to see a stereoscopic illusion and some cannot see them at all. If you are finding it difficult, try holding the book close to your nose, so the image is out of focus, and slowly move it away without refocusing your eyes on the page.

Follow the instructions on page 100 to discover what is hidden in these stereograms.

Can you see a star?

Can you see a heart?

SPOOKY!

Can you see a plane?

3-D HAND

Create a fantastic 3-D image of your hand to fool all your friends. It's easy to do, although it will take a little patience. You will need thick colored felt-tip pens and a piece of white cardboard.

"EYE-POPPING" ACTIVITY!

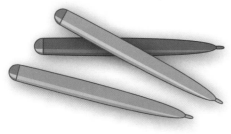

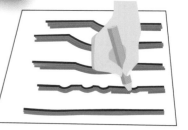

3 *Build up lines of color, following the contours of the black lines, using different colors of pen.*

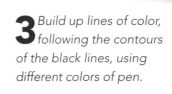

COOL!

1 *Draw around your hand with a pencil on the cardboard.*

4 *Continue until you have filled in the whole hand. Cut off the edges of the white paper to make the illusion look truly awesome.*

2 *Using a black felt-tip pen, draw a straight line up to the edge of the hand outline, then a curve across the hand to the other side, then another straight line, as shown. Repeat 4 times, at equal distances from the top to the bottom of the hand outline. Remember to put a curve across each finger of the hand.*

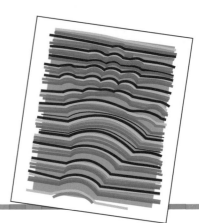

CHAPTER 8

ILLUSIONS EVERYWHERE

Optical illusions don't just belong in books. They are all around you—in nature, on the streets, and even in your own home. Keep your eyes open and see how many you can spot.

FACES ALL AROUND

Take a look at all these photos. At first glance they all show very different subjects. But look again ... They all have something rather peculiar in common. They should all remind you of faces.

This entry phone in Venice even has eyebrows.

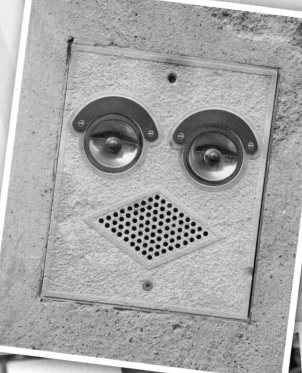

This wide-mouthed car was snapped at the Chicago Auto Show.

AWESOME!

The cone of Mount Fuji looks like white hair as it rises up above the staring eyes of this roof in Japan.

Look at this telescope. Can you see eyes, a nose, and two ears that stick out?

What happens?

Our brains are programmed to recognize faces from the day we are born, so it's not surprising that we see them wherever we go. See how many you can spot at home and when you're out and about.

POINT OF VIEW

Sometimes nature's own optical illusions are caught on camera, producing unusual images that are not quite what they seem.

Is this a two-headed giraffe?

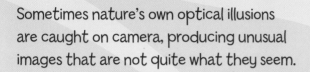

This zebra appears to have one head and two bodies.

The cloud passing above this tall smokestack looks just like white smoke.

SEEING IS BELIEVING

Stand in front of the bathroom mirror, then hold up a hand mirror in front of you so it faces the bathroom mirror too. How many "yous" do you see? You probably see too many of you to count. This is because the hand mirror reflects the reflection in the bathroom mirror which reflects the reflection of the hand mirror... and on and on!

WEIRD!

DISTANT SHOTS

Here, clever camera tricks have been used to create some funny fake photos.

The mirror in this photo has been positioned to reflect the top of the photographer's head, creating an intriguing image.

IT'S INCREDIBLE!

SPOOKY!

The man in this image is perfectly aligned with the woman's mouth—and as he is standing some distance away, he appears to be just the right size for a quick snack.

Snappy illusions

Many tourists take the opportunity to show off their strength by "supporting" the Leaning Tower of Pisa. Try making use of perspective by taking some trick photos of your own. You could show a friend pretending to lift an impossible weight with one hand or standing next to a "giant" animal.

"EYE-POPPING" ACTIVITY!

NATURE'S TRICKS

Wind and water often sculpt rocks into strange shapes. Can you spot the animals suggested by these fantastic formations?

Hvitserkur rock in Iceland is all that remains of an ancient volcano. The sea has carved holes at its base, giving it the appearance of a giant creature taking a drink.

This bird is often said to hide its head in the sand, but in this rocky representation it is hiding its body instead.

This jumbo-sized creature is not normally found in the desert.

SEEING IS BELIEVING

COOL!

Is Anyone There?

In the animal kingdom, staying hidden can be an advantage for both predators and their prey. Here are some of nature's most impressive masters of disguise.

SEEING IS BELIEVING

Can you spot a frog on this tree trunk? The mossy frog lives up to its name. It is found in Vietnam, where it hides on rocks and trees.

Believe it or not, this is not a piece of seaweed, but a leafy seadragon. This relative of the seahorse is found off the coast of Australia.

AMAZING!

You might struggle to see the orchid mantis in this picture. Its shape and color exactly match the petals of the flower it is sitting on.

Street ART

Two-dimensional chalk drawings can create really convincing 3-D optical illusions when viewed from the right angle.

HOW DO THEY DO THAT?

If you look carefully, you can see the two artists completing this 3-D illusion, which was part of a festival of street art held in Chiang Mai, Thailand.

Like many 3-D street illusions, this drawing gives the impression of a hole in the ground. It was created for a street art festival in the Dutch city of Almere.

STRETCH IT OUT

Take a look at this painting of the English king Edward VI, painted in 1546. Viewed from front on it looks completely distorted.

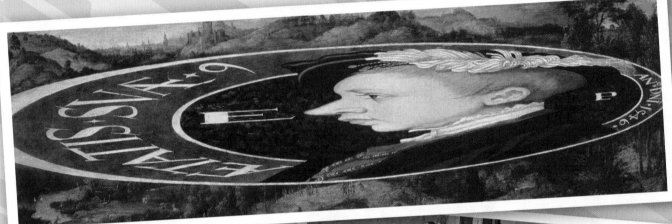

Now look at the painting from the side. All of a sudden it looks normal. This is an example of anamorphic art.

What happens?

Anamorphic art is a distorted image that is created to be viewed from a specific vantage point. The word anamorphic comes from Greek— "ana" means "back" or "again", and "morphe" means "shape" or "form."

Many examples of street art are anamorphic images. Here a street artist adds the finishing touches to an image of the Beatles. Can you see how exaggerated the perspective is?

Now look at the same image from the correct viewing point.

WOW!

Trompe L'Oeil

Trompe l'oeil murals are optical illusions that are painted onto walls. The words "trompe l'oeil" mean "fool the eye" because the murals fool the eye into seeing an image in 3 dimensions.

This mural on a wall in Quebec City, Canada, was painted by 12 different artists. Historic figures appear in the windows, together with some of the city's leading artists and writers.

Tell me more

William Michael Harnett was a master of trompe l'oeil painting. The 19th-century American artist painted life-size objects with such convincing detail that it is hard to believe they are not real.

120

AMAZING ART

In most art galleries, people are not allowed to touch the works on display and photography is strictly forbidden. But at this trick art show visitors were encouraged to interact with the 3-D paintings—and to take photos of the very funny results.

UNBELIEVABLE!

This father and son show no fear in the jaws of a terrifying Tyrannosaurus rex!

WEIRD!

IT'S ALIVE!

In this amazing painting the tiger appears to be stepping out of the picture frame into the real world. Notice the tiger's shadow painted on the gallery wall.

HOW DO THEY DO THAT?

AMAZING!

I DON'T BITE!

It looks as if this marine monster is swimming right out of the painting and about to grab this young man's head in its fearsome jaws! The cleverly positioned "shadows" on the wall and the picture frame help to make the illusion work.

AWESOME!

BENDING LIGHT

Light can create optical illusions when it bends as it passes through glass or liquid. The pencil in this glass is perfectly straight where it enters the drink, but it looks as if it is broken.

What happens?

When rays of light travel from air to water, they slow down, in the same way that we walk more slowly through water. When this happens the rays bend where the two materials meet. This is called **refraction**.

BENDING SPOONS

You can create your own light-bending optical illusion with just a spoon and a glass of water. Here's how to do it.

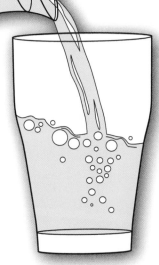

1 *Half fill a glass with water as shown above.*

2 *Place a spoon in the glass of water.*

3 *Look at the glass from the side. Does the spoon appear to be broken where it enters the water?*

"EYE-POPPING" ACTIVITY!

WEIRD!

SEEING IS BELIEVING

AMAZING MIRAGES

Have you ever seen a shimmering patch on the road that looks like water from a distance, and then found that there's nothing there? What you saw was a mirage and they don't happen only in the desert.

This picture shows a mirage in the desert.

What happens?

Mirages are optical illusions. On hot, sunny days, light beams bend as they move from cooler air to warm air close to the ground. They bounce up toward your eyes making you see a reflection that looks like water.

SEEING IS BELIEVING

Look closely at this picture. Can you see a thin blue line just above the surface of the water? This is called a fata morgana mirage. Fata morgana mirages appear in a narrow band above the horizon. It happens when the surface temperature is colder than the air above it, and is normally seen over water or areas with ice or snow on the ground.

CREATE YOUR OWN MIRAGE

This experiment will allow you to create a "mirage" of your own. You will need a picture or photograph, a large glass, a pitcher, salt, and water.

1 *Ask an adult to boil some water. While it is still hot, dissolve as much salt in it as you can. Then let it cool.*

2 *Pour the cooled salt water into the glass. Put some fresh water into a pitcher and gently pour it on top of the salt water. You need to keep the layers of salt and fresh water separate for the illusion to work. You could try pouring the fresh water over the back of a spoon to avoid disturbing the salt water layer too much.*

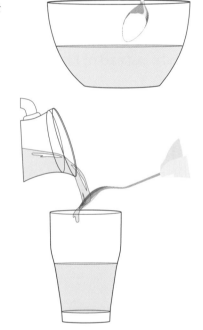

3 *Place the photograph behind the glass of water and look at it through the glass. What happens?*

WEIRD!

What happens?

You should see a mirage as the light is refracted (bent) differently as it passes through the salt water layer and the fresh water layer.

"EYE-POPPING" ACTIVITY!

GLOSSARY

Afterimage An image that stays on the retina after the eye has stopped looking at it. People often see afterimages after looking at bright lights. Afterimages can be positive or negative.

Binocular vision Using both eyes together to see a single image. The slight difference in angle between the view from each eye makes it easier to judge distances.

Color assimilation The effect that a color has on a neighboring color. For example, red looks more orange when it is next to yellow and more purple when it is next to blue.

Concentric Concentric circles all have the same center point, no matter what size they are.

Cone cells Cones are short, thick nerve cells in the retina that specialize in seeing bright lights and colors. Cone cells do not work well in low light, which is why we cannot see colors very well when it starts to get dark.

Contrast The difference in brightness between two colors that are next to each other.

Horizontal Running from left to right.

Lens The lens in the eye focuses light rays on the retina. It changes shape depending on whether we are looking at something close up or far away.

Mural A painting on a wall.

Negative (image) An image showing colors that are reversed from the original: for example, white instead of black.

Parallel Lines or objects that are side by side with the same distance between them.

Perspective The appearance of things compared to one another according to their distance from the viewer.

Positive (image) An image showing colors that are the same as the original.

Pupil The dark circle in the center of the eye that allows light to reach the retina.

Refraction The bending of light as it moves from one substance to another.

Retina The back part of the eye that contains the rod and cone cells.

Rod cells Rods are long, thin cells in the retina that are super sensitive to low levels of light. Rod cells help us to see in the dark and are good at seeing the shape of objects.

Stereogram An image with another 3-D image hidden within it. It's created by incorporating two images taken from slightly different angles into the same image.

Tesselated A pattern made of identical shapes that fit together without any gaps.

Three-dimensional (3-D) An object that has height, width, and depth, such as a cube.

Trompe l'oeil This is French for "trick the eye." It refers to paintings that create the optical illusion that objects and scenes are 3-D.

Two-dimensional A flat object that has height and width, but not depth, such as a square.

Vertical Running from top to bottom.